Where We Belong

Madeline Sayet

T0179942

methuen | drama

LONDON • NEW YORK • OXFORD • NEW DELHI • SYDNEY

METHUEN DRAMA
Bloomsbury Publishing Plc
50 Bedford Square, London, WC1B 3DP, UK
1385 Broadway, New York, NY 10018, USA
29 Earlsfort Terrace, Dublin 2, Ireland

BLOOMSBURY, METHUEN DRAMA and the Methuen
Drama logo are trademarks of Bloomsbury Publishing Plc

First published in Great Britain 2022

Cover design: Jade Barnett

A catalogue record for this book is available from the British Library.

Library of Congress Control Number: 2022935123

ISBN: PB: 978-1-3503-3879-1
ePDF: 978-1-3503-3880-7
eBook: 978-1-3503-3881-4

Series: Modern Plays

Typeset by Mark Heslington Ltd, Scarborough, North Yorkshire

To find out more about our authors and books visit
www.bloomsbury.com and sign up for our newsletters.

Acknowledgements

This play would never have existed without the collaboration, love, and support of so very many people.

As with most things in my life, much of this play was created from conversations with my mother, without whose creativity, inspiration, and guidance I would never have become a writer.

Thank you to my father, who no matter how many times this play was performed, still felt it was his responsibility to show up. As he always does for his children.

Thank you to Erik, for standing by me, even on those days I wanted to flee rather than tell this story – you reminded me that I had something important to say.

Thank you to director Mei Ann Teo, who agreed to direct this play when it was half as long as it is now, with no idea what it might be but always led by a fierce curiosity about how the story we were telling was changing us as we moved through it.

Thank you to Vera Starbard, for being the best dramaturg, confidant, and question asker as we traveled along this path together.

Thank you to Maria Goyanes, who believed it was a play before it was one, and that it should be shared with as many people as possible.

Thank you to Michael Walling, for understanding the importance of Native stories, and your work sharing them in the UK.

Thank you to Michael Whitmore and the Folger Shakespeare Library for your belief in the publication of this work.

Thank you to Asa Benally, for weaving good medicine into every fiber of my costume.

Thank you to Hao Bai, for helping us imagine how we move between the earth and sky.

Thank you to Erik Schilke, for flawlessly scoring this journey with brilliance, subtlety, and nuance.

Thank you to Madeleine Hutchins, Tara Moses, Kenny Ramos, Erin Tripp, Emily Preis, and Delanna Studi for being the most incredible workshop cast of versions of myself. Thank you for speaking my words, so that we could hear them and dig deeper together – And to Hutchins in particular, having another Mohegan be a part of this project's development has at each stage made it all worthwhile. It truly could not have happened without you.

Thank you to jb for capturing the film adaptation and helping us all understand the sky a little better.

Thank you to Mekala Sridhar for understanding that it is not a play but my actual story that needs to be cared for in different ways.

Thank you to Grace Chariya for traveling across the country with me, holding this show. The title 'Stage Manager' does not begin to cover your role in this.

Thank you to my friends, scholars, and collaborators in the UK, who carried me through my years overseas.

Thank you to my agent Michael Finkle and the producing team at Broadway and Beyond Theatricals for your work sending this show across the country.

Thank you to the ancestors who join me every night to tell this story, and remind me that what we pass down is important.

Thank you always and forever to the late great William S. Yellowrobe Jr., for making a place for Native artists in the theater, and teaching us that it is in fact where we belong.

Production History

Early Development
The space organizations offer for readings and development are key to creation. *Where We Belong* exists because the following theaters opened their doors to us early on.

The first time any words from this play were read was in the lounge at Dixon Place, NY, in January 2018.

In July 2018, a section of *Where We Belong* was read as part of Global Female Voices at the Arcola, in London, produced by Global Voices Theatre. (This is how the Origins Festival found out about the work.)

In November 2018, the first full draft of *Where We Belong* was read on the set of Larissa Fasthorse's *Thanksgiving Play* at Playwrights Horizons as part of their Indigenous Voices Series curated by Emily Johnson.

Larissa Fasthorse has given each theater she works with the requirements that: She cannot be the only Native work in the season, and she cannot be the only Native person paid. This set up the landscape not only for this reading to happen, but also for a theater culture willing to accept accountability riders like the one required with this tour.

In February 2019, Rattlestick Playwrights Theater provided space to workshop the play, and in December 2019, hosted the first reading in America after the London performance.

Woolly Mammoth Theatre Company continued this support by allowing for workshops in which Sayet could hear the work read by other Native Theater artists.

An earlier version of *Where We Belong* was first presented in June 2019 at The Sam Wanamaker Playhouse at Shakespeare's Globe in London as part of Border Crossings' ORIGINS Festival, the UK's only large-scale multidisciplinary festival of Indigenous arts and culture.

Playwright and Performer: Madeline Sayet

Director: Mei Ann Teo
Costume Design: Asa Benally

In 2021, Woolly Mammoth Theatre Company in Association with The Folger Shakespeare Library produced a film adaptation of *Where We Belong*, recorded in April 2021 and released in June 2021.

Playwright and Performer: Madeline Sayet
Director: Mei Ann Teo
Dramaturg: Vera Starbard
Production Design (Lighting and Scenic): Hao Bai
Costume Design: Asa Benally
Original Composition and Sound Design: Erik Schilke
Director of Photography and Editor: jb
Stage Manager: John Hall

In October 2021, Woolly Mammoth Theatre Company re-adapted the show for live performance with Baltimore Center Stage.

In April 2022, Woolly Mammoth Theatre Company in Association with the Folger Shakespeare Library launched a national tour of *Where We Belong*, premiering in April 2022 at Philadelphia Theatre Company

Playwright and Performer: Madeline Sayet
Director: Mei Ann Teo
Dramaturg: Vera Starbard
Production Design (Lighting and Scenic): Hao Bai
Costume Design: Asa Benally
Original Composition and Sound Design: Erik Schilke
Stage Manager: Grace Chariya
Technical Director: Megan J. Coffel
Standby for Madeline Sayet: Emily Preis
Dialect Coach: Liz Hayes
Casting Director: Judy Bowman
Executive Producers: Broadway and Beyond Theatricals

2022 Touring Locations:

Philadelphia Theatre Company, Goodman Theatre, Hudson Valley Shakespeare, Seattle Rep, The Public Theater (NY)

Woolly Mammoth Theatre Company

Woolly Mammoth creates badass theatre that highlights the stunning, challenging, and tremendous complexity of our world. For over forty years, Woolly has maintained a high standard of artistic rigor while simultaneously daring to take risks, innovate, and push beyond perceived boundaries. One of the few remaining theatres in the country to maintain a company of artists, Woolly serves as an essential research and development role model within the American theatre. Plays premiered here have gone on to productions at hundreds of theatres all over the world and have had lasting impacts on the field. Co-led by Artistic Director Maria Manuela Goyanes and Managing Director Emika Abe, Woolly is located in Washington, DC, equidistant from the Capitol Building and the White House. This unique location influences Woolly's investment in actively working towards an equitable, participatory, and creative democracy.

Woolly Mammoth stands upon occupied, unceded territory: the ancestral homeland of the Nacotchtank, whose descendants belong to the Piscataway peoples. Furthermore, the foundation of this city, and most of the original buildings in Washington, DC, were funded by the sale of enslaved people of African descent and built by their hands.

The Folger Shakespeare Library

Folger Shakespeare Library is the world's largest Shakespeare collection, the ultimate resource for exploring Shakespeare and his world. The Folger welcomes millions of visitors online and in person. It provides unparalleled access to a huge array of resources, from original sources to modern interpretations. With the Folger, you can experience the power of performance, the wonder of exhibitions, and the excitement of pathbreaking research. The Folger offers the opportunity to see and even work with early modern sources, driving discovery and transforming education for students of all ages.

The award-winning **Folger Theatre** in our nation's capital bridges the arts and humanities through transformational performances and programming that speak inclusively to the human experience. Folger Theatre continues its legacy through exciting interpretations and adaptations of Shakespeare and expands the classical canon through cultivating today's artists and commissioning new work that is in dialogue with the concerns and issues of our time. Folger Theatre thrives both on its historical stage and in the community, engaging audiences wherever they happen to be. Learn more at folger.edu

Mei Ann Teo (Director) is a queer immigrant from Singapore making theater and film at the intersection of artistic/civic/contemplative practice. As a director/devisor/dramaturg, they create across genres, including music theater, inter-medial participatory work, reimagined classics and documentary theater. They helmed *Dim Sum Warriors the Musical* by Colin Goh and Yen Yen Woo, composed by Pulitzer Prize winner Du Yun for a national 25-city tour in China. Recent work includes Jillian Walker's world premiere *SKiNFoLK: An American Show* at the Bushwick Starr, Madeline Sayet's *Where We Belong* at Shakespeare's Globe and Woolly Mammoth and the North American premiere of Amy Berryman's *Walden* at Theaterworks Hartford. Teo received the League of Professional Theatre Women's Josephine Abady Award and is the Associate Artistic Director and the Director of New Work at Oregon Shakespeare Festival.

Hao Bai (Production Designer) is a multidisciplinary designer in lighting, sound, video projection, and world-building (environment) for live and virtual performances.

Recent: *Virtual: Final Boarding Call* (Ma-Yi Theater+WP Theater); *Nocturne in 1200s* (Ping Chong). Lighting: *Waterboy and the Mighty World* (Bushwick Starr & The Public Theatre). Projection: *Electronic City* (NYIT Awards). Sound: *Walden* (TheatreWorks). Upcoming: Production Design: *This Isle is All* (Harvard). Lighting/Projection/Sound: *Arden* (The Flea). Lighting: *CHINOISERIE* (Ping Chong). Sound: *Little Shop of Horrors* (St. Louis Rep).

Asa Benally (Costume Designer) is a Citizen of the Navajo and Cherokee Nations. *The Rez Sisters* (Stratford Festival); *Venus & Adonis, Savitri, CAV + PAG* (New Camerata Opera); *Grounds* (International Contemporary Ensemble); *Sweat* (Center for Contemporary Opera); *Mrs. Warren's Profession* (The Gingold Group); *Blues for an Alabama Sky* (Keen Company, Drama Desk Nomination); *Somewhere Over the Border* (Syracuse Stage); *Too Heavy For Your Pocket* (George Street Playhouse); *Skeleton Crew* (Westport Country Playhouse); *Measure for Measure* (The Public Theater Mobile Unit); *Cymbeline* (Yale Repertory Theater); *The Brobot Johnson Experience* (The Bushwick Starr); *Whale Song* (Perseverance Theater); *The Winter's Tale* (HERE Arts Center). Training: M.F.A Yale School of Drama. B.F.A. Parsons School of Design. Online: www.asabenally.com

Erik Schilke (Composer and Sound Designer) is an ambient electronic composer and music producer. His debut album Synthesis was recently released on the German label Hymen Records. He has previously scored film projects for acclaimed directors including Fernando Lazzari and Madeline Sayet. Online: erikschilke.com and *hymen-records. bandcamp.com/album/synthesis*

Vera Starbard (Dramaturg) *T'set Kwei yóo x̱at duwasáakw. Vera Starbard áyá ax̱ saayí. Dleit áa x'éináx̱ Vera Marlene Bedard yóo x̱at duwasáakw. Teeyneidi naax̱ x̱at sitee. T'akdeintaan yádi. Wooshkeetaan dachx̱án. Dena'ina dachx̱án. Takjik' ẖwáan áwé uháan. Shaan Seetx̱ x̱at ẖuwdiztee. Dgheyaytnux' ẖux̱aa.óo.* Vera

Starbard, T'set Kwei, is a Tlingit and Dena'ina writer and editor. Her mother is of the Teeyeineidi clan and her father is T'akdeintaan. Vera is Playwright-in-Residence at Perseverance Theatre through the Andrew W. Mellon National Playwright Residency Program and Editor of First Alaskans Magazine. Vera is also a writer for the PBS Kids animated children's program 'Molly of Denali,' which won a Peabody Award in 2020. Vera currently lives with her husband Joe Bedard (Inupiaq/Yup'ik/Cree) on the Dena'ina land around Dgheyaytnu – colonially called Anchorage, Alaska. www.verastarbard.com

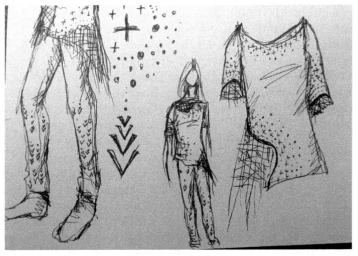

Costume sketch by Asa Benally.

Madeline Sayet is a Mohegan theater maker who believes the stories we pass down inform our collective possible futures. She has been honored as a Forbes 30 Under 30 in Hollywood & Entertainment, TED Fellow, National Directing Fellow, NCAIED Native American 40 Under 40, and a recipient of The White House Champion of Change Award from President Obama. She serves as a Clinical Assistant Professor at ASU with the Arizona Center for Medieval and Renaissance Studies (ACMRS) and is the Executive Director of the Yale Indigenous Performing Arts Program (YIPAP). Her plays include: *The Neverland*, *Antigone or And Still She Must Rise Up*, *Daughters of Leda*, *Up and Down the River*, and *The Fish*. Recent directing work includes: *The Neverland* (Krannert Center, Illinois), *Tlingit Christmas Carol* (Perseverance Theatre), *Midsummer Night's Dream* (South Dakota Shakespeare), *Henry IV* (Connecticut Repertory Theatre), *Whale Song* (Perseverance Theatre), *As You Like It* (Delaware Shakespeare), *The Winter's Tale* (HERE Arts), *Poppea* (Krannert Center, Illinois), *The Magic Flute* (Glimmerglass), *Macbeth* (NYC Parks), *Miss Lead* (59e59).

www.madelinesayet.com

Introduction

In Mohegan culture, we have a symbol, the Trail of Life, that depicts the ups and downs of life, and the people you meet along the way. This symbol is embedded in much of the stage design of *Where We Belong*, because what you are about to encounter is a journey along the trail, no more no less.

This was never meant to be a play. When I arrived home from London in the spring of 2018, my feet didn't stick quite right to the earth anymore. It was a truly disturbing feeling as a Mohegan person. Every time I had ever arrived home prior to that, it was as if I could feel my roots reaching down from my toes all the way through the earth. Suddenly, everywhere I landed, I felt distant, as if I was watching the world from above. It was as if I had truly become my namesake – the blackbird. So I began to write out my thoughts in order to grapple with some questions.
Questions like:
As a Mohegan person, does missing England make me a traitor?
How are borders created?
Is it possible to be both a bird and a wolf?
As an Indigenous person in a globalized society, is there a place where I get to belong?

What I was writing was never meant to be shared with strangers, and yet in grappling with these questions, I found there were thoughts, ideas, and moments in my own journey that resonated with others.

So I hope whether you first encounter this story onstage, or in this book, that you carry with you whatever resonates, particularly any questions it raises for you about your own life.

I also hope you take the time to learn more about my people, and the Indigenous peoples of whatever lands you occupy.

But most importantly, for every Indigenous person reading or in the audience, know that your story is powerful and has as much right or more to be told on stage.

Image by jb.

Each Presenting Theater Had to Agree to the Following Accountability Rider Developed by Woolly Mammoth Theatre Company with Playwright Madeline Sayet

WHERE WE BELONG TOUR
TOWARDS COMMUNITY ACCOUNTABILITY:

If not already in existence, Presenter agrees to develop a plan to authentically engage in a continuous, long-term relationship with the Indigenous people whose land they occupy and/or the urban Indian/local Native population. It is important to both Madeline Sayet and Woolly Mammoth that this tour not become its own colonial force but rather encourage current relationship between theatres and the Native peoples whose land the theatre occupies.

This plan would include all of the following:

a) Highest levels of the organization committing to an initial dialogue with Producer (Woolly Mammoth) and Performer (Madeline Sayet) about the organization's history and relationships with local Native communities. Producer commits to provide initial resources and guidance on relationship building based on Presenter's needs, with periodic follow-up conversations to discuss progress.

b) Incorporation of a Land Acknowledgement in presenter's programs, website, public spaces and/or pre-show announcements, and best efforts for this to be kept up in perpetuity by the organization for all productions. Presenter would make the following public commitments (on social media, website, and/or in the production press release) as a measure of accountability.

c) Public acknowledgement of past instances of redface at the institution, and commitment to not present any programming in the future which includes redface.

d) Public commitment to provide opportunities for Native artists within their programming for future seasons.

Presenter agrees to curate the following public programming in connection with *WHERE WE BELONG*, through partnerships with local Native communities:

e) Centering the work of a local Native playwright or writer (poet, essayist, comedian, lecturer, etc) through a stand-alone event in association with *WHERE WE BELONG*. If a local Native writer cannot be identified then another art form would be acceptable, but a writer is strongly preferred. Ideally, this writer is from the Native community whose land the Presenter's theatre resides.

f) An event, discussion, or lobby display created in collaboration with local tribes amplifying the Indigenous languages of that land, paired with an encouragement to donate to local language revitalization efforts.

g) Distribution of complimentary tickets for *WHERE WE BELONG* to Native people; to include both single ticket buyers and larger groups organized through partnerships with Native community leaders, and cultural and/or arts centers. Presenter commits to providing a travel subsidy to larger organized groups to be used for the form of transportation best suited to their needs.

h) Community Meet-and-Greet that brings together the artist and crew, with those intimately connected to the Presenter (to include organizational staff, leadership, Board, etc.) and the local Native population to engage in a dialogue about the people, and the place where the show is being produced. Ideally, this event also involves some other form of shared experience, such as a meal.

Presenter understands that Woolly Mammoth and Madeline Sayet will not undertake this community engagement work on behalf of the presenting theatres, unless where otherwise specified above.

NOTE ON THE PROLOGUE OF SHOW: Each tour stop will be getting a new prologue for the Show from the Author, with specific reference to the Native communities in that local area. This can also incorporate language about whatever specific collaboration is happening between the theatre and local tribes, and honor their language on their land.

Agreed & Accepted:

Presenter

By:_____

Title: _____

Where We Belong

This play is dedicated to Mohegans past, present, and future.

Setting

The Earth – Old, hurt, carved with lines by foolish people

The Sky – Free, expansive, beyond all else

The River – Focused, alive, ever changing.

Time

Four Hundred Years: 2016–2021 and 1620s–2021, and yet no time at all.

Prologue

This moment is outside of the 'play.' Each performance location has its own intro that grounds us in the place the story is being told, and the story of that place.

Baltimore Opening: In 1707, Nansonnan, chief of the Piscataway, demanded justice for her daughter – because the constable had robbed her daughter's grave. Baltimore is on the traditional lands of the Piscataway, and yet it's likely many of you have never heard of them, or knew there were female chiefs here before the advent of the United States. My friend, Piscataway historian Dr. Gabrielle Tayac, told me about this powerful Piscataway woman, Nansonnan. And her demand for justice. I do not know if she received it. It's not my story to tell. You must speak with the Piscataway to learn their stories, the stories of this land.

It is thinking of Nannsonan and the many strong Native women who have stood here since then, that I share my stories with you today.

Borders

So . . .

Lights shift. It's as if a world of story possibilities exists before her.

Where do we need to start today?

A line appears.

Ah, okay.

Lights shift.

I'm standing in a queue at a border. Fucking queues. To enter Sweden. It's June 24th 2016 and I'm at the airport in Stockholm. And it's a short line, which is a sign I'm entering Sweden and not the United States. But the line is going oddly slowly.

When I get to the front of the line, I realize it's because the question the man is asking each passenger getting off the plane from London is *not*: 'What is the reason for your visit to Sweden?' As is customary at borders.

I think I misheard – I'm sorry, what?

With a wry smile and awareness of the power of his position, as gatekeeper to a country, the question he is asking is:

'How did you vote in the Brexit referendum?'

. . . I couldn't vote. I'm not British.

'How would you have voted? Remain or leave?'

I guess I would have voted remain.

He smiles, nods, right answer. Lets me through.

She crosses the line, it disappears.

. . . And for a moment, I'm relieved. I'm relieved because I agreed with the right side, the safe side, in this particular instance. But the safe side is different. Depending on which line you are trying to cross.

Today the word remain means togetherness, tomorrow it could mean apart.

No one talks about anything else all week. Every non-British person warily eyes their British coworkers – Which ones voted us gone?

Five short months later, America elects Donald Trump President.

America and England have revealed their roots. They do not believe all people are created equal, they never have.[1]

---

[1] The American Declaration of Independence both states that 'all men are created equal' then continues on to make clear that not all people are included in that, by referring to Native people as 'merciless Indian savages,' within the same text. The country was founded on white supremacy, and those who do not fit within its terms, are often still fighting to be considered 'people' under the law.

Borders get more and more intense. Fucking queues. The lines do not get shorter.

Another line appears in front of her.

A few days later, I'm back in London at the machine that scans my fingerprints to make sure I am still who I was the last time I entered the country. Feeling oddly protected by this device that says: I do in fact belong.

The Border Guard looks up –

'Hiya, what's the reason for your visit to the UK?'

I'm a student here.

'What do you study?'

I'm doing my PhD in Shakespeare.

'Oh really, PhD, that's a long time, ya?'

She nods.

'I studied him in school.'

Oh, yeah? (*She smiles supportively.*)

(*He clears his throat.*) 'Is this a dagger that I see before me?'

He gestures dramatically as if cradling Yorick's skull.

That's pretty good. (*She's lying.*)

From behind me, 'Did you hear that? She's studying Shakespeare in England, how exciting!'

The border guard hands me back my passport and visa, 'Cheers.'

She steps through/over the line.

I don't tell him I'm also studying colonialism. Most people don't like talking about colonialism as much as they like talking about Shakespeare.

I spend a lot of time at this gate. At a lot of gates. They all look and feel the same. Lines drawn in the sand by petulant children with guns.

Border queues always feel like waiting in line to get in trouble.

Do you belong? Do you? Who decides?

I feel I am supposed to be here less often than I am and I wonder if anyone will ever notice, or if the lightness of my skin and my knowledge of Shakespeare mean I will never really get questioned for anything.

The line disappears.

In the States, I direct plays. As a Native person, I promote Native stories. In the UK, I study Shakespeare. My area of research is the relationship between the Indigenous peoples of America and Shakespeare's plays.

Today's story isn't about Shakespeare though.

It's not a traditional Mohegan story either.

Today's story: is how I became a bird.

A Wolf Named Bird

Aquay tonkutayuw. Nuwisuwonk Sgayo Jeets. (*Shakes head.*) Chuh. Nutuyooees Acokayis.[2]

My name is Acokayis. I am a Mohegan.

Those are the first words I was taught to say in Mohegan and I was taught to introduce myself that way everywhere to make sure Mohegan is always being spoken. Somewhere. That it's never really a dead language. That our ancestors

---

[2] The performer introduces herself twice, moving between different orthographies of the Mohegan language, as they changed between 2006 and 2021. This happens throughout the play. It's reflective of her relationship to the journey the language has taken up until the moment in her life of the story's telling.

still hear it every so often, and you remember the ground on which you are standing.

My mom taught me in the Mohegan language: you can leave your nation, but you can no more leave the land from which you are from, than you can your leg. There are no words for that, the place you are from is physically a part of you.

My English name is Madeline Fielding Sayet. The Fielding is for Fidelia Fielding/Flying Bird/Jeets Bodernasha, the last fluent speaker of the Mohegan language. My mom never wanted me to be able to forget the importance of our language, or of Flying Bird's work to preserve it, so she wove Flying Bird's spirit into both my English and Mohegan names.

So that there could never be a day I wouldn't think about our language.

Beat.

Ya, no pressure.[3]

My Mohegan name, Acokayis, means blackbird or the dark one who flies apart.

She looks up at the sky.

I've been spending more time in the sky lately. Alone.

Mom says it's dangerous –
'You have to be careful. You can't keep going up there. The sun spews radiation at you when you go up there and you'll die. You'll get cancer and die.'

I tell her America has the third highest rate of cancer in women in the world, but that is not as concerning to her for some reason.

---

[3] Humor is very present in the performance of this play, on the page it reads more subtly, but it's important for the reader to know that the tone of this work is not all somber and academic, and that it is intentionally working against what audiences have been trained to think Native people are like.

She calls: 'Where are you?'
Home.
'Why didn't you call? I was worried.'
Why, Mom? Did something happen?
'No, I just kept thinking – you're so far away across the sea.
When are you coming back home?'
I sent you my schedule.
'You sound sad, are you sad?'
No, Mom, I'm fine. I just got home and need to settle in.

We hear music.

It keeps happening.

As the music comes in, something shifts in her physicality. This is the beginning of how we understand her journey with the sky.

I keep ending up in the sky. And all this sky time, all this looking down. It's changing my relationship to Mother Earth. To who I am.

Back on Earth.

Two Households – Both Alike In How To Lock A Door

As a kid, I hated flying. Weird, for someone who is about to become a bird. When I was 9, my older sister took me to see *Final Destination*. Do you know that film?

She asks the audience directly, and if they respond she works with their responses.

Yeah, so an entire school trip to France explodes at take-off and anyone who survives is now on a list to DIE based on where they would have been sitting on the plane. It's now their destiny.

So – I see this film as a kid and the sky and DEATH are now instantly synonymous in my mind.

If I fly I will die – simple as that.

For some reason my parents don't understand the level of commitment I have to this idea. They decide I am going to go with my father to get on a plane – ON THANKSGIVING – a day already rife with tension. For a FUNERAL. This is really not a good omen. So, I decide I am DEFINITELY NOT. My life is at stake.

And I come up with a plan.

My parents come from different cultures and are already divorced at this point – so Thanksgiving traditionally consists of two very separate meals.[4] To symbolize the division in my family. We do lunch with my mom's family for Thanksgiving #1, the one with Natives, and dinner at my dad's for Thanksgiving #2, the one with Jews. Today, there is a high probability I can make use of the inherent distrust and confusion between parents to execute my plan.

So – the minute my dad rings the doorbell –
I march straight upstairs –

She runs upstage, and becomes more and more the child version of herself.

and lock myself in the only bathroom there is absolutely no way to open from the outside. SAFE!

She ducks low to the floor and a line appears on the ground in front of her.

They look for me. They realize where I am. They beg me to come out. But they can't get me out! The screaming outside quickly devolves into whose fault it is that I am in here.

I'm sitting on a border war between two feuding households and the law says I have to go with him, but I'm not going anywhere. I'm safe behind my locked door.

---

[4] The play does not explore the nuances of the history of Thanksgiving, but instead uses the holiday to illustrate its continuing tie to divides. In reality, this 'holiday' is very complex, and the playwright's sister, for example, prefers to participate in *Day of Mourning* each year rather than Thanksgiving. National Day of Mourning does not celebrate the arrival of the pilgrims, but instead remembers the genocide of Native peoples that occurred due to their arrival.

I brought a notebook in with me.
They pound on the door, they offer bribes, they threaten punishments.
I simply pass notes under the door explaining my reasoning:
I don't want to die.
I don't want to die.
I'm not getting on a plane, if I do I will die.
If you really want to die, you can go ahead and get on a plane without me, but I'm not going to.
I'm not going in the sky! It's too dangerous.

The child version of herself fades away, and she continues to reflect, but now from the present.

My dad and siblings give up and get on the plane without me.
My dad doesn't usually drink, but I'm told he ordered a shot of vodka and yelled at my siblings for letting me lock myself in there.
I bet he really thought it was Mom's idea.
In his shoes I would have needed more than one drink.

I was a nightmare child that day (*She stands back up.*) – but fear is a powerful convincer. Especially when you can control the locks.

The line disappears.

For years, I was named bird, but would not fly. I did not want to. Mohegan actually means wolf people. We're wolf clan, always have been from wayyyy back. Wolves don't fly. They don't need to.

What's In A Name?

My Mohegan wolf family was really all about staying put. They wouldn't leave. Like at all. As elders, my Aunt Gladdie and Uncle Tom stopped leaving home altogether. They were terrified that if they left, they might die somewhere other than on Mohegan Hill.

Which let me be clear – to my family – is THE WORST thing that could happen.
Our medicine relies on being home, being where our ancestors can look after us.

Aunt Gladdie – Medicine Woman Gladys Tantaquidgeon – was a living legend. She founded Tantaquidgeon Indian Museum with her brother and father at the height of the Great Depression on the idea: 'It's hard to hate someone you know a lot about.' Together they protected our stories and other sacred relations, like pipes and baskets, within our Museum, where it was warm and dusty and always smelled like good medicine.

But you see outside of Mohegan Hill –

She steps across a line.

To be Native in CT is basically to be told every day that you don't exist, and decide whether or not today's the day it's worth fighting about. As a kid, my mom or other Mohegans would show up at my school to intervene and make sure our history was being taught correctly. But as a teen, my mom is constantly reminding me it's now MY responsibility to fix things. If I falter for just one moment:

She becomes her mother, pointing a harshly judgemental finger.

'Sooooo, you're acting white! Are you a white person now?!'
No, Mom.
'This is your responsibility! You know that! Did your ancestors sacrifice for nothing?'

Noooo, Mom.

So, on those days when my mom makes sure I go and tell my teachers to their face that I will *not* be handing in their assignment on Manifest Destiny from the settlers' perspective, but *will* in fact be writing a paper on Wounded Knee so *they* learn something – I take comfort in knowing no matter how much trouble I'm caught in . . . I can escape (*she runs away*) . . . to Shakespeare rehearsal. And be someone else.

We hear music heightening the moment.

'Oh Romeo, Romeo, wherefore art thou Romeo? Deny thy father and refuse thy name, and – *I'll no longer* be a Capulet!'[5]

The music abruptly cuts out.

You know? Normal teen stuff. And in Shakespeare I don't have to worry about making a mistake or saying the wrong thing, it's already written. He has words for what I don't. For things I feel but can't express without him. I know that if I can just shed my skin and become Juliet, *be* Juliet, people will love me. Speaking these words, I become a part of something hundreds of years old that makes people feel alive.

So 'teen me' splits my time between performing for a local Shakespeare theater and working for my tribe.

I'm at the tribal offices, updating some Mohegan language documents with one of the elders and my mom, who, after Aunt Gladdie's recent passing, has just been appointed the new Medicine Woman of our tribe.

We have been working to revive our language, but with no living fluent speakers, it's a complicated reconstruction process relying on written documents. I love our language and stories and have been finding phrases in Mohegan to include in plays we are creating with the Mohegan youth.

The elder I'm with suddenly stops short –

'Wait, what's your name?'

Sgayo Jeets. Blackbird.

'Huh.'

---

[5] I'm not citing this. You all know what it is.

The elder scrolls through the document in front of her.

The dark one who flies apart.

'Sgayo . . .?'

I was named after Jeets Bodernasha. Flying Bird.

The elder is still looking at the papers.

'No, that can't be your name. There must have been an error in the translation.'

No. That's my name. That's been my name my whole life.

'No, no. Hmmm, Sgayo would be the conjugation for the inanimate.'

An inanimate blackbird? So I am dead!?

My mom jumps in, 'Ohhhh, that kind of makes sense actually, the bird you were named after was dead.'

Mom, what!?

'I told you this!'

No, you definitely did not tell me this. You definitely did not tell me that I was named after a DEAD BIRD. I thought I was named for birds flying IN and OUT of the house when I was born.

'Yeah, and one died. In the house. Then your Uncle Tom had to pass, because someone's spirit had to go with the bird, and we were all worried it would be you because I just had two miscarriages.'

So I am a DEAD blackbird!?

'No, no, that's not how the language works.' The elder brings us back to the reality at hand. 'You can't even put those two words together. It wouldn't mean anything at all.'

She opens the language dictionary to find the right word for a *living* blackbird – because our language was killed and has to be resuscitated – APPARENTLY JUST LIKE ME.

They find the right word. Both the elder and my mother start giggling uncontrollably – completely unconcerned with my growing desperation.

What's so funny?

'The word . . . is suks-uh-kok.'

WHAT!?

'Suks-uh-kok.'

They find this very amusing.

Suks-uh-kok Jeets!? That sounds like a porn name! Why would you name me that!? There has to be another word!!!

They look, still giggling – 'Acho-kayis?'

That sounds like a sneeze.

'Well, it's better than Suks-uh-kok.'

. . . And it's true anything is better than Suks-uh-kok.[6]

On paper, I become a bird again. This time a live one. But this name does not feel tied to me. Not really. What I've lost in translation is so much more.

She shrinks down and kneels with the audience for a moment.

I was named for Jeets Bodernasha, Flying Bird, the last fluent speaker of the Mohegan language. The woman who kept speaking it even when there were no living people left that she could speak it to. She still spoke it to the ancestors, the Makiawisug,[7] wrote it down.[8] Back then everyone

---

[6] This shift in awareness and orthographies in this scene occurred at the time of the creation of the 2006 Mohegan-Pequot dictionary. Since that time, which orthographies are used has shifted again, with developments in the language reclamation project. The initial orthography was a combination of the work of Fidelia Fielding and white anthropologist Frank Speck, who – ironically and inconveniently – had a notoriously bad ear for the Algonquin language family to which Mohegan-Pequot belongs.

[7] The Makiawisug are the little people of the woodlands. Mohegan people leave gifts for them in the woods, and Flying Bird was known to have a close relationship with them.

[8] Fidelia Fielding/Flying Bird kept journals in the Mohegan language.

thought she was crazy. Now, I don't have Jeets in my Mohegan name anymore.

I'm not even really sure what it means now . . .

And I can't be sure I won't lose it again.

I look at my wings, wondering if they'll ever work, wondering if they even know what they are.

The settlers killed something in our souls when they took our language. My whole life I've been waiting for the day we can say it's back. Really fully back. And we don't have to trip on our own tongues, on our own minds, to express ourselves anymore. But every step toward reclaiming it is a complicated battle against the world that wanted it gone.

I take comfort in words I can understand:
In plays
In Shakespeare
In language society cares about, unlike my broken language.
Shakespeare makes me normal.

She resumes her teen identity, but uses Shakespeare's text to be about her own situation.

'O be some other name. What's in a name? That which we call a rose by any other name would smell as sweet, so'[9] –

I take comfort in knowing I can go to Shakespeare rehearsal, FALL IN LOVE, and DIE. The teenage dream. Right?

On a school trip to the theater . . . I finally see a Native character enter the stage for the first time. But they aren't played by a Native actor. Instead a non-Native enters the stage, in redface, treating ceremony and medicine as if it's a joke. My classmates laugh louder and louder. (*She shrinks.*)

---

[9] Dear Shakespeare nerds, this is not an incorrect quote. The variation of 'word' and 'name' in the third sentence is a discrepancy between Q1, 'a rose by any other name' and Q2 and the First Folio 'a rose by any other word.' This is done intentionally as a play on the fact that even printings of Shakespeare have textual variations and are not static.

What do they think is so funny? Would they laugh that way at me if I told them how I felt? I tell my mom what I saw.

'You'll see a lot of that, I'm afraid. Too many have been taught wrong about us. That's why it's our job –'

I know, I know. To fix it.

I trade the pressures of home for a train away to Manahatta to study theater. A living bird on a speeding train, away from my wolves and the words lost in translation, to the land of skyscrapers. But climbing buildings doesn't teach you how to fly. It's hard to rest in a place with no trees.

I run into the occasional psychic who reminds me that there are others traveling with me, and I nod. Uncle Tom, Aunt Gladdie. Flying Bird. We all have ancestors at our backs.

We can sense the ancestors around her.

They tell me New York isn't where I'm supposed to be, but I'm not ready to fly yet. I don't know where they are sending me.

You Taught Me Language

I spend *a lot* of time with Shakespeare. A language that I don't have to worry about losing. I find my voice in Shakespeare, my friends in Shakespeare, even my love in Shakespeare. I come back to it again and again. Inside it, I can transform. Whatever it is I have to say, when I speak Shakespeare people listen.

My favorite play is *The Tempest* because it makes me feel like maybe Shakespeare could actually see me, just around the corner. A new world coming. What might he have thought as he read those descriptions of our world only an ocean away, as he wrote in 1611.

I wish others could see what I see.

Every time I read it, see a production, I feel they've gotten something horribly wrong. Don't they understand that Shakespeare is anti-colonial?

That this play is about here, about us. About what the world once was and the possibility of what it could be. If this is our only representation in the canon, surely Shakespeare wouldn't want them to do what they've been doing?

'This island's mine by Sycorax my mother, which thou takst from me.'[10]

Caliban is no monster.
He's Indigenous.
He's me.

It's the only play I think about directing. Something is left unsaid. I must prove it. I must prove them wrong!

I stare madly at another portrayal of a Caliban who babbles like a fool onstage. As if he never spoke at all. As if his language wasn't more complex than his colonizers. As if he was not Prospero's equal or better. What would people learn if Caliban could only get his language back!

What would happen if Caliban *could* get his language back? If . . . as he moved toward freedom his language came back too, replacing that of his oppressor . . .

She moves from a place of questioning to the excitement of imagining and creation.

If Ariel, the airy spirit, too was of here, was blackbirds like me, a flock of blackbirds, everywhere and nowhere at once – if their language was my language. And this was a story of something that happened here long ago. After all, in the play, the settlers leave the island at the end. Maybe I can prove Shakespeare wanted the colonists to leave too.

---

[10] Act 1, Scene 2 of *The Tempest.*

'You taught me language, and my profit on't is, I know how to curse.'[11]

And suddenly I've done it! I've made my production!
If Shakespeare was anti-colonialism –
Shouldn't we all be?

Academics love it.

'Ah yes,' they say, 'this is what *The Tempest* was always about.'

I realize the power that comes with showing people a different way of seeing the world.

'This is clearly what *The Tempest* was always about.'

It's clear now. Isn't it? Leaving the island at the end of the play means Shakespeare wanted the colonists to leave too. To go back to England.

So I can't help but imagine: what if they had . . .

The First Divide

Mohegans, we have a complicated relationship with the English.

A lot of colonized peoples have a complicated relationship with the English.

Ours begins in 'friendship.' True betrayal requires trust. As Mohegans we descend from Chief Uncas, known historically (to the colonizers) as Uncas, 'friend of the English.'

Yeah, and that's right, I said *we* descend. He had A LOT of children. Contrary to what that *Last of the Mohicans*[12] nonsense would have you think.

---

[11] Same Caliban speech in Act 1, Scene 2 of *The Tempest*.
[12] In *Last of the Mohicans*, James Fenimore Cooper combined the Mohicans in upstate New York and the Mohegans in CT to create his fictional tribe. Then, by making our leader, Uncas, the last of his fictional version, he killed us all in the minds of most people with the stroke of a pen.

Early 1600s, we are all Pequot. One nation. Living together along the Massapequotuck, the river we call home.

We are transported to the river together.

White strangers arrive on our shores. They aren't like us. They think differently, have different values. You see, long ago, we used to practise peacekeeping over warring, because we knew wars are unwinnable. There is only ever loss. But now our leader, the chief of the Pequot, wants to fight these strangers. But a sub-chief, Uncas, believes we will all die if we fight.

Who would you side with?

Fight the outsiders! Protect our children! Preserve our ways of life at any cost!

OR

Make peace with these strangers and hope that we can still build trust.

Most of our nation cannot fathom the amount of oncoming change. We should fight the English, keep things the same. Fight for and hold onto what we love.

But Uncas, he's seen the way these strangers fight.
They are brutal. They don't care about balance, stability, community, peace – they care about *winning*. It's not normal. The English will do whatever it takes to win.

We can't fight them. The only way to survive is to make peace with these strangers.

But as a nation,
as a family,
we aren't all in agreement.
Our tribe breaks in two.

A line appears, she must cross it.

Many stay, but a small group of Pequots follow Uncas across the Massapequotuck river and form a new tribe taking back the Pequot tribe's old name from long ago –

Mohegan
Wolf people.

We ally with the British.

War begins between the Pequots and the British. The
Pequots are actually doing really well for a while, but the
British, you see – they want to win. So in the night, while the
chief is away – they burn the Pequot village to the ground,
massacring everyone in their homes and shooting anyone
who tries to escape. Only a few children survive.[13]

The Mohegans, we all survive – protected by the side of war
we chose when we thought we were choosing peace.

Is this war now? Is war killing children? Our cousins . . .

Nothing could be worth this. How can they not understand?

What will keep us alive?
War or peace?
Leave or remain?

In the ashes of the British fire that burned his cousins to the
ground: What did Uncas see?

Be like Uncas,
I was told growing up,
make friends for your people.

We would never have survived without him, we say. We love
him. We will always love him. He was faced with an
impossible choice for his people.
And we survived.

---

[13] Between 500 and 700 Pequot men, women, and children were massacred in their
homes on May 26, 1637. This indiscriminate killing was unlike any type of warfare the
Pequot had ever encountered. Prior to that, for the first eight months of the Pequot
War, the Pequot won every battle. The English, however, would stop at no lengths, and
celebrated this horrific massacre. The Governor declared the massacre, 'A day of
Thanksgiving,' which highlights why that word and holidays created in its name carry
so much trauma. To this day, there is nothing in that spot acknowledging what
happened there.

But I've always wondered – what would have happened if we had allied with our people instead?
Is there a world in which we could have defeated the English together?

It's strange but the white men only ever wrote down what our *men* were doing. They didn't think our women were important. Our women have always led us, continue to lead us, even at this moment we have a female chief and medicine person. But the English, they couldn't fathom this, so they only wrote the history of what *they* could identify as leadership.
The men, the battles.
They didn't know it was truly only our women who could decide if we went to war. . .

A Changing World

Back in New York, I find myself amidst generations of incredible Native Theatre artists who with little funding and great imagination have been telling our stories onstage. Amidst them, now, as a director, I can lead rehearsal rooms full of only Native artists, where the cultural protocols are our own. I do what I can to promote Native theater – build partnerships, make friends with the larger white institutions, in the hopes we can reach more people. Producers start calling – (*excited*):

'We read your article!'
'We've heard about your work.'
'We'd love you to do a Native version of a classic.'
'No, we don't want anything *specific,* just Native-y y'know generally.'
'Something *our* audiences can relate to.'
'Feathers, fringe. Some Native flair.'
'It's just a story! There's no reason to be sensitive about it!'

'No, we don't need *Native* performers, we'll just dress them up to look Native!'
'Clearly we were wrong about you –'

VOICEOVER: They don't care about balance.

'– we'll be making some changes to your show –'

VOICEOVER: stability, community, peace.

'– for commercial reasons.'

VOICEOVER: They care about winning.

Despite everything Uncas sacrificed for their 'friendship,' the English colonists do not uphold their treaties.

There is a growing divide between the English colonists and the English nation.

Here at home, the colonists start stealing our lands. They re-name our Massapequotuck river, the Thames. But for some reason it gets pronounced Th-ames.[14]

She moves toward the water.

To appeal to the English leaders directly, more than one of my ancestors must now cross that vast ocean on diplomatic missions to that faraway place in service of our people – to try and fix things.

But they don't get to fly.
It's not time yet.
The ocean carries them instead.

To fly, we have to forget ourselves.
Our limits.
To fly we must be carried by the wind.
You need a lot of ancestors on your team to get a good wind.
And you have to listen to them to know where you are going.

---

[14] They do not listen to the land and what it wants to be called when they arrive, but instead try to carry with them names of places from their old world. The phonetic difference here is that of the British and American pronunciations of Thames.

I need a fresh start. Somewhere I'm not hated for being me.

I look across the ocean to the place where the words I can speak fluently come from.

Wishing I had the others, but knowing they will never fully come back. I need to be able to use these living words.

I have to change. Mohegans, wolf people, we don't leave. Not unless we have to. You can't speak it in our language. It would be like saying you left your arm or your leg behind. You don't leave a part of yourself behind unless something very bad happens.

Maybe if I can just get back to Shakespeare, I'll have the language I need.

If I can just get back to Shakespeare, everything will become clearer.

Alright.
I am going to the UK to study Shakespeare!

But as the words leave my lips my mom shoots back – 'Why? Do you want to be white?'

No, I don't want to be white. I just want to be a part of something I'm good at. Shakespeare isn't only for white people.

'But you want to study a *white man*?'[15]

No, I'm not studying the man – the white man – I am studying the ongoing life of his work –

'AND you have a ZIT – see this is BECAUSE you want to study a white man. It's bad medicine.'

She thinks everything is bad medicine.

---

[15] Many of the scenes in this play are taken verbatim from conversations in my life, but this scene is not actually composed solely of words spoken to me by my mother. The beginning of this scene is created from responses some members of the Native theater community had to my decision. My mother is a tribal leader, so it feels important to note that she did not actually say this.

Mom won't stop though, 'Do you know what it's like to dedicate your life to the survival of a small group of Indians in Connecticut. To know that your mission is our survival?'

Yes, Mom.

'Then WHY are you running across the ocean to study a white man?'

I'm not running! This is what I'm really good at. This is how I can help!

'We must ALL stand in love for the tribe.[16] That is the only way we will survive.'

But what if we don't? What if I do what you say and it still all ends? What if I can't stop it? What if in my lifetime we all just fade away?

Mom takes in a long deep breath.

'Then you will have to explain that to your ancestors when you face them. Mmm hmm. When they greet you, at the end of this part of your journey. If you're still enough right now, you can hear them already.'

I close my eyes and listen. Listen for the voices of the ancestors between worlds.

Am I running?

Or is this my chance to do something important?

What should I do?

She can hear the ancestors chatter around her. She opens her eyes and steps forward.

I board the plane like everyone else – but as the plane begins to move, something new takes hold of me. Fear does not guide my decisions, the way it once did.

She begins her transformation.

---

[16] On March 7, 2005, on the eleventh anniversary of Mohegan Federal Recognition, when asked if she had any words for her people, Medicine Woman Gladys Tantaquidgeon said, 'We must all stand in love for the tribe.' She was 105 years old at the time. It has become a multi-generational lesson of great import.

I close my eyes and suddenly imagine: I am the plane. And the plane is a bird. And the air under our wings, the dips and dives and curves of the wind all there supporting us – carrying us higher and higher into the sky. Take off.

Suddenly we are in the sky – it's unlike anything we've seen before, expansive, above and beyond, free.

Flying becomes a blessing.

When I come down I am far away in a strange land.

She lands. The sky is gone, we're in England.

The air is softer here, people take time to sit and drink their tea, the workdays are shorter, the holidays longer, so people can spend time with their families. Everyone has healthcare. And companies can't put poison in your food. It's so different from what I imagined.

How come America can't agree on these basic rules to take care of each other?

I'm here to study Shakespeare. With other people who love Shakespeare. I've always been really good at understanding Shakespeare. This is my chance to be a part of something that matters!

She looks around and realizes how alone she is.

But there are no other Mohegans here . . .

So I cling even more to Shakespeare! Try to bury myself in Shakespeare. Pull out meaning in his verses, fill his words in order to exist, but the more time I spend with him – the more –

The Shakespeare cuts in like a weapon.

'You taught me language and my profit on't is –'

As she moves through this scene she shifts between embodying the academics offering a barrage of questions and herself trying to counter them.

'What do you think about *Caliban? Caliban? Caliban?*'

Ban, ban, Ca-Caliban, get a new monster, make a new man.[17]

Well I think it's important in contemporary conversations that Indigenous peoples not be confined to only being a part of Prospero's subconscious. Also, have you ever noticed the only characters who refer to him as a monster are the ones trying to sell him?

'We should incorporate something from your culture into this piece, y'know something *primitive? Primitive? Primitive?*'

No, I'm not sure what you mean by that. My culture is actually incredibly complex.

'We're so glad that you're uniquely positioned to write about the experience of *The Native? The Native? The Native?*'

'The Native' is a trope. There is actually no singular version of Indigenous peoples. We are all unique.

'Why should someone who is an expert in *English literature* be up to date on the correct terms for *race*? They're separate fields after all.'

I am still. I am still. I am still. And I close my eyes to listen but the ancestors feel so very far away.

What would my people want me to do?

I will change things. I will change things. I will change things. I will show them we are human.

'Talk about *The Tempest! The Tempest! The Tempest*! Talk about the-talk about the-talk about *The Tempest*!'

Um, well it was the first show I ever directed . . .

'How perfect.'

She is crushed and exhausted.

---

[17] Text is a variation on Act 2, Scene 2 of *The Tempest*.

Seeking Justice From The Crown

I'm wandering down the cobblestones of the South Bank of their River Thames by London Bridge. An alien on alien shores.

There are no other Indians around to talk to about what's wrong.
Why a story should only be told in a way that heals the community, never in a way that hurts it.
Why you shouldn't take the seats in the front if there are elders coming.
Why no one here knows colonialism happened,
or are proud of it.
It's even weirder than the fake version of history in American textbooks.
This tea time on an island far away with no awareness of the many many massacres that industry was founded on is eerie.
I want to go home.

The air thickens,
sky darkens,
it begins to pour.

We hear the rain.

I duck into Southwark Cathedral for shelter. There's an otherworldliness to these old churches. I always wonder who the builders were. The space has a majestic quality that makes me feel like I'm not supposed to ask that.

The rain stops.

When it stops raining, I poke my head out into the backyard of the cathedral. There's a garden. I wind my way down along the stone path to the back of the garden where I can see a large rock. Isolated in the middle of a grass circle. The rock feels familiar.

I move closer.
The trail of life is carved on its edges.
Curving up and down.

By the rock is a sign.
'Mahomet Weyonomon, Sachem of the Mohegans, is buried in this churchyard.'

Next to the stone plaque, a familiar type font and a story with the title, 'Seeking Justice from the Crown.'

(*She reads.*) Mahomet Weyonomon came here in 1735 seeking Justice from the Crown for the unfair treatment of his people.

I find family I forgot was here. He wasn't much older than me.

Aquay, Mahomet.

'Awán nah yôksqá?'[18]

Achokayis. (*Beat.*) Did you get justice, Mahomet?

'No, there was a queue.'

Fucking queues. How long?

'Few months, long enough for me to get smallpox and die first.'

But you came all the way here?

'Yea well, that didn't mean as much to them as I thought it would. I thought being a leader, coming to see another leader – that that would still mean something.'

Wait – so after all that – they didn't see you? What were they just like – Oh well that's too bad. You see, our leader is a very important person, and there's a queue.

'Yup. So I waited. And that was my life's journey. Waiting for an audience that never arrived.'

Why are you buried *here*? Why can't we bring you *home*?

'They don't know where in the graveyard I'm buried. This wasn't Southwark Cathedral then. It was just where foreigners got dumped. *Foreigners* weren't allowed to be

---

[18] Translation: Who is that girl?

buried within city limits and this was just across the river. Easiest place to ditch a body.'

At least they put you on the water. Traditional.

'If they'd known that they probably wouldn't have. Didn't get any of our people visiting for hundreds of years.'

2006, I remember now, Tribal Council came, brought you this rock, this bit of home from Mohegan.

'Ya. The queen came and everything. I guess they aren't as busy now. (*beat*) Rocks. Rocks are important in our culture. Our word for leader – Sachem – it means rock person. Some of us stay with the pack and take care that way, others are meant to travel alone. It can be a great sacrifice to be a rock person, but we hold space and make a great impact just the same. Hey, qustamooôk!'[19]

(*She laughs*) Yeah, sorry. I'll bring some next time.

VOICEOVER: We must all stand in love for the tribe.

I am grateful for my friend. I return with tobacco and sit with the only other Mohegan in London, this rock – when I need comfort. I speak Mohegan to him. He hasn't heard it in hundreds of years. He doesn't tell me I speak it wrong. I write about the dangers of redface in my research, and the Shakespeare scholars tell me they are confused that I seem to have a problem with 'dressing up' so I come and tell Mahomet about it. He gets these things.

She stands and slowly begins to move away from Mahomet, working through her thoughts.

I need to write.
That's why I'm here.
What is it I need to write about?
Why did I think Shakespeare was anti-colonial?
Because I believed he was good or because I needed him to be? Does it matter? Maybe there is something between

---

[19] Translation: Tobacco.

Shakespeare and home that I can use to show them – we are more than what they think of us, than what's been stolen.

Who Are We When We Fly?

Once people find out I am studying Shakespeare in England, I am asked to tell stories all over. Every time I tell a story, someone else asks me to fly. I fly more and more often until I spend as much time in the sky as on the ground.

We are in the sky, expansive, free.

Each time I fly, I look down at things my ancestors never saw and my descendants may not get to. The whole world. I look down at the ice sheets of northern Greenland, awestruck at the fragility of our home.

Even at its most terrifying, the sky brings me peace. A sense of distance, moving between places, people, ideas. The rules down there seem so fluid, subjective, now in a way I could never see up close. Nothing is concrete.

But the more time I spend up here in the air, the lighter my feet fall when I land. Is it possible to be both a bird and a wolf?

I land. (*We're back on earth.*)

I'm at TED Global, listening to a talk on the global commons.

The speaker is standing on their red circle announcing – 'everything on this planet we share. The resources and the trash. There is only this one planet that we all share.'

Ask literally any Native person ever and they coulda told you this. This is supposed to be an expert – did they really just figure this out?

Someone nudges me – 'Hey, I heard you cast Native people in your Shakespeare productions! How innovative!'

Is it? Why would I imagine a world where I didn't belong?

Another person butts in – 'Oh you're a Shakespeare person – did you know that Shakespeare is how Starlings first got to America?

Uh, no, I did not.

'Oh, ya! A huge Shakespeare fan tried to introduce all of the birds referenced in Shakespeare's plays to Central Park! Really messed up our ecosystems. That's how we got one of our most dangerously invasive species. Now they've expanded all the way to California, regularly destroying the habitats of indigenous birds.'

(I'm not exactly sure how the Starling reference in H41 is inspirational, let alone motivation to kidnap the poor birds and bring them to a new country.[20])

Another fellow asks me where I am from:

I am Mohegan, but I live in London.

'Ahhhhhh, you are a bit British then now.'

Nooo, the British are the colonizers of my people, so I'm not British, I'm Mohegan.

'You've been living in London. You're a bit Londoner now, we become a bit of every place we live.'

I argue – until the next talk begins –
This one is on the way the market benefits from dividing us. How each moment, we are being encouraged to choose sides in everything we do.

Maybe I am becoming a bit Londoner . . . Does being a bit Londoner make me a traitor?

I long for a world without sides.

---

[20] *Henry IV Part 1*, Act 1, Scene 3. This scene with Hotspur is the reason the birds were brought here.

London is a big city, but I have family there. Mahomet's been there longer than I have been anywhere.

Does that make him British now?

I cross oceans. I wonder what he has learned.

Leaders are rocks. I tell myself. Leaders Are Rocks.

The Mohegan Man Who Believed In The Words Of The Bible

Frustrated, she comes downstage, begins to drink water, and chats to the audience.

What am I missing? Where can I look to understand how all of this connects?

As she is drinking water a book falls from the sky, surprising her. She picks it up, and opens it.

Occom! Of course. He crossed the ocean not long after Mahomet. As far as Mohegans go, he's pretty famous. The first Native writer to ever have his words published in the English language. It's a big deal. It means he's the first Native voice we have writing back – *in books.*

She opens the book, and begins to read.

At 17, Samson Occom found God.

She turns back to the audience.

That's the same age I found out I was a dead bird.

She lets the physical book carry her on the journey moving between it and the audience, as music comes in and picks up, bringing energy to that journey.

He becomes a minister, believing that Christianity and education will help Native people. He's inspired to found an Indian College in Connecticut, when the white minister

Eleazar Wheelock encourages Occom to cross the ocean to England to raise the funds.

Where were you, Occom? What happened? Where can my feet take me that match up with your footsteps? Could you have been at Garrick's Shakespeare Jubilee? Did you preach in Stratford? Did you preach . . . Everywhere? Where can I find you?

1766.

She jumps into Occom's voice.

'Sin. Sin has made man devilish and beastly. Yea, he is sunk beneath the beasts, and is worse than the ravenous beasts in the wilderness. He is become ill-natured, cruel, and murderous. I say he is worse than the ravenous beasts, for *wolves* do not devour their own kind, but man does.'[21]

Occom travels across England delivering between three and four hundred sermons in less than a year. (*Beat.*) Three and four hundred? Damn. I thought my lecture schedule was busy.

He draws huge crowds everywhere he goes.
Donations pour in.
His dream – the Indian college – will soon be a reality.
Change is coming.

King George III receives him at court and even donates to the effort.

As Occom's fame increases, there are plays making their way onstage in London in which –
White actors parody his efforts.
But it doesn't matter. Occom's raised more than 12,000 pounds. That's more than three million dollars today![22]

---

[21] From 'A Sermon preached by Samson Occom at the Execution of Moses Paul: An Indian' Sept 2, 1772. This quote is used out of historical context to give a sense of Occom's preaching style.

[22] It was recently 3.29 million, but inflation has been varying widely – so please feel free to look up what 12,000 pounds from 1770 is today, if you want an exact figure.

He survives the rough trip back across the ocean to Mohegan!

He arrives home to find –
The school's charter is changed.

1771

She becomes Occom navigating Wheelock's betrayal.

'Your having so many white scholars, and no Indian scholars at the school gives me great discouragement. I verily thought once that this institution was intended purely for the poor Indians, with this thought I cheerfully ventured my body and soul, left my country, my poor young family, all my friends and relations, to sail over the boisterous seas to England to help forward your school, hoping that it may be a lasting benefit to my poor Indian brethren. But when we got home: behold all the glory had decayed.'[23]

The funds build Dartmouth College, on stolen Abenaki land in New Hampshire.

Something breaks in Occom. He leaves Mohegan. He leaves for good.

She wanders away, lost, she is both herself and Occom as she speaks the next line.

Can you imagine back to a world before all of this? Before it was all torn apart? Come away with me, beyond the reach of the white man. Together we will start over.

There is no point in petitioning the King this time . . . The colonists no longer think they are English.

The Revolutionary War approaches, changing the rules again.

Back home on Mohegan Hill, it's not long before President Andrew Jackson's Indian Removal policies threaten to tear

---

[23] Letter from Samson Occom to Eleazor Wheelock, July 24, 1771.

us all from our homelands. But Lucy Teecomwas[24] founds
Mohegan church with her daughter to prove we are
christianized and civilized so that we can stay. They each give
up a piece of their land for the church and write a clever
deed that states as long as there is one Mohegan living the
church will always be Mohegan land.

It is the only piece of our traditional lands that we never
lose.

The Mohegan Ladies Sewing Society secretly passes down
our customs at the church for generations.

VOICEOVER: We must all stand in love for the tribe.

What Is Home?

I Skype my mom:
'Wow, you look terrible. Come home.'
No, I can't just come home. I'm here doing work.
'Hmmm?'

*Mom begins going through the motions of smudging her through the
Skype.*

Mom. Mom, what is that?

Smudging.

Are you trying to smudge me through the Skype?
'Uh huh.'
Does that even work?
'Gotta be better than nothing.'
They said I have to stay here two more years.
'So come home!'
That would mean quitting the PhD.
'Ya, come home. Just get an honorary doctorate.'
It's not that simple.

---

[24] Lucy Teecomwas was Samson Occom's niece. Lucy Occom Tantaquidgeon was
Samson Occom's sister. Lucy Teecomwas was her daughter.

'Your aunt Gladys got two honorary doctorates for doing
work for our people. She came home.'
Mom, I can't just –
'Then write faster.'
I can't!

And I start to wonder if I know what home means
anymore . . .

The Mohegan Girl Who Believed In The Power Of Shakespeare

*She crosses toward the audience. And begins to drink water and
chat, as she works through her thoughts.*

I need to write. Something. Occom. Mahomet. Uncas.
Everything that came after. We are so much more than the
fucking *Tempest*. Than what Shakespeare could imagine us to
be.

He never met us. Never heard our stories. Our language.
He didn't know we didn't use curses . . . then. And wouldn't
have claimed the island 'mine.' We don't need Prospero's
book for power! We have our own way of seeing the world
they can't define. But could open their minds . . .

There is possibility in Shakespeare's poetry.
I read the plays and imagine *us* into the stories.
All of them.
Not just *The Tempest*.
We can't be confined to who we might have been in his
mind.
If we are going to be taught these texts, we have the right to
interpret them for ourselves.
To indigenize Shakespeare!
Shift what is centered,
focus on the stories' relationship to the lands they are being
told on.
Translate them into our own languages.

Center relationality,
the earth,
our ways of thinking
and point out and question the colonial violence in the plays.
There must be a way to write about that.
To show them the difference
between who we are
and how they see us.

We are suddenly at a lecture.

In order to talk about Indigenous Shakespeares though –
We have to go back to *how* Shakespeare got to America, to
Indigenous peoples.
We have to talk about erasure, genocide, and assimilationist
education initiatives in America designed to eradicate
Indigenous cultures and replace them.

You may not know that both Dartmouth and Harvard were
originally founded as Indian Schools –

'No.' A voice spits back.

What do you mean no?

'That is surely erroneous.' The critic scoffs.

It is in their charters, you can't just say no because it offends
your understanding of the world. Many many schools of all
grade levels were founded to educate and assimilate Indians.
We know Shakespeare was taught as part of some of these
assimilationist schools for several reasons.

A woman raises her hand, 'I thought you were going to tell
us about your love of Shakespeare?'

VOICEOVER: You taught me.

I am! One way we know Shakespeare was taught at Carlisle
Indian School, one of the residential schools that children
were stolen from their homes and taken to, is that one

student – when forced to give up his name for a new English name – took the name Will Shakespeare.[25]

She throws an imaginary spear in resistance.

More hands go up. 'I thought you were going to talk about Native Shakespeare productions –'

VOICEOVER: You taught me, taught me.

I am! But the context is key. The exciting Shakespeare productions in Indigenous languages in the 2000s, they come out of language reclamation movements. You don't have a language reclamation movement until after a language removal process.

Imagine you are a child, stolen from your home from everything you know, taken somewhere far away with terrible living conditions, and when you try to speak your language, the one way you have of expressing yourself – you are beaten for it. You try again and you're beaten harder – because they don't want you to express yourself. They want you to become like them. So you learn to speak English to survive. The government thought it was so important that our cultures be removed and be replaced, they didn't care how many thousands of Native children died at the schools. That's a part of the legacy of how we came to speak Shakespeare, so –

'But, you love Shakespeare, yes?'

VOICEOVER: You taught me language and –

I do!
I do. But that doesn't mean his work isn't also used as a tool of colonialism.

'How do we make people love him the way we do!?'

VOICEOVER: And my profit on't is –

You don't have to do that . . . He's not intrinsically superior. We are allowed to love other things.

---

[25] William Shakespeare, citizen of the Arapahoe Nation, was a Carlisle student in 1881.

The lecture fades away, and she feels alone and small once more.

My career began because I created a show that asked: What would happen if Caliban could get his language back?

Would anyone have *cared* about those Mohegan words – if they didn't come from *Caliban*?

By the early 1900s our language is seen as useless. Flying Bird is the last fluent speaker. She keeps a journal, in which she writes in Mohegan so the future generations might have it. But she's the last to live it. To speak it fluently, to be able to speak to our ancestors and the spirits of the woodlands correctly. By the end of her life, everyone thinks she's crazy for holding onto a dream that may never come true.[26]

VOICEOVER: We must all stand in love for the tribe.

I fly. I land.

A line/border appears.

Mahomet and Occom can never come home. Their spirits are in London and at Oneida[27] now . . . but Flying Bird stayed and the world still slipped out from under her . . .

I fly. I land. (*A line/border appears.*)

There's nowhere to go.

VOICEOVER: We Must All Stand in Love for the Tribe.

But, what if everything I know fades into the darkness!?

What does it mean to be a wolf named bird in a place far from home?

---

[26] Anthropologist Frank Speck borrows Flying Bird's journals, and the majority of them burn up in a fire at his professor's house. Flying Bird dies believing that all of her journals have been destroyed. It is only after her death that a few additional journals are found.

[27] Occom is buried in upstate New York on land that the Oneida gave to the Brothertown Indians. The Brothertown Indians are the tribe that was formed when a group of Native people from several nations, including Mohegan, Pequot, Narragansett, Niantic, Tunxis, Montauk, went west with Samson Occom.

Indians In Boxes

An academic has asked if we can meet up at the British Museum. He wants to know my thoughts on the North American section – the Native American exhibit.

She steps forward as if entering the museum, the space becomes colder around her.

On the way in we stop through the British section, a celebration of the height of empire. He gestures enthusiastically, 'Here's the shield of the first aborigine killed when Cook arrived in Australia! There's a repatriation claim[28] on it,' he notes, 'but they're not giving it back.'

No . . . instead they are displaying their crime proudly.

He looks up disdainfully, 'We have a problem with migratory birds coming in here and staying because it's warm.'

My mind flies up high to where they're resting.

She looks up.

He continues – 'They always leave a couple dead ones behind and it takes ages to find the bodies . . . it's a real nuisance.'

She looks back down. She reads.

'This museum was set up to examine civilizations. It's the third most popular museum in the world.'

Do you have British things here?

He shrugs.

'Some, but that's not really what we're known for. Here we go. North American section.'

The space shifts drastically, now full of lines and tormented spirits.

---

[28] Repatriation is when sacred items are returned home to their peoples, particularly with the understanding that these objects carry spirits with them, and they belong with their people like any living being. In this instance, a 'repatriation claim' means that the return had been asked for but not granted.

I step back. Giving the sacred relations space.

'How did these get here?' – I ask – looking at a mash of mislabeled Indigenous artworks, like varying nations crowded into a rail car – a continent facing genocide over hundreds and hundreds of years – wide expanses of geography thrown together in cases without specific acknowledgement.

'Oh, they take "legally acquired" very seriously.'

She moves slowly, carefully, through the room of sacred stolen relations.

I make an awkward path through the room, aware that many of them are still alive and have been displayed without awareness of their medicine and power. Living objects like these that carry spirits with them, they hold space on their own, and my feet awkwardly pattern out their natural borders.

Legally acquired – meaning?

'The objects have been purchased. It doesn't extend beyond that.'

Have their peoples asked for their return home? Are there repatriation claims on any of these?

'Oh yes,' he nods, 'Also on a couple of human remains.'

The air becomes tight.

You don't return human remains?

'No, no, not so far.'

What exactly does *legally acquired* mean?

'Ah well,' he fiddles for the right words, 'it doesn't take into account the circumstances of purchase so if they were starving and had to sell it –

or if Americans killed our relatives for the highest fee and sold them to the highest bidder –[29]

'We could buy them, yes. As long as they were "purchased" by the museum.'

You have other people here too? Not just Native Americans, right?

He nods.

'We have a ton of Maori trophy heads. Recently, a Maori artist wanted them displayed under a structure he built, so that we could show the world what we had done. I thought it was very exciting. Museum didn't go for it, naturally.'

But, I mean everybody? Not just my peoples? Not just Indigenous peoples, *everybody's* peoples.

'Yes, the collection is extensive. Asian Pacific Islanders, African, extensive mummies.'

How many *people* do you think you have in storage here in total?

'How many human remains?'

Yea, how many *people*?

He tries to count, 'Well, not including hair, there was a whole thing about whether or not hair counted –'

Okay, not including hair.

'Probably about 12,000. Not including hair.'

12,000?

---

[29] Colonial and American policymakers often offered bounties for the scalps of murdered Native people. In 1703 The Massachusetts Bay Colony offered £60 per Native scalp. In 1724, the New Hampshire legislature offered £100 per male scalp, £50 for women. In 1755, the Phips Proclamation offered £50 for the scalps of Penobscot men over 12, £25 for every woman, and £20 for every child under 12. The derogatory term 'red-skin' was often used in association with this practice. *The Daily Republican*, in Winona, Minnesota, Sept 24, 1863 reads, 'The state reward for dead Indians has increased to $200 for every redskin sent to purgatory.' This practice continued for hundreds of years. These are just a few of hundreds of instances in which settlers became rich murdering Native people.

The presence of the spirits in the room swells around her.

You have 12,000 people here. And you won't let them go home?

'No, if we start giving back human remains, well they don't know where that would lead. They might have to give other things back.'

Where do you draw the line between things and people?

'No, they don't really. That's the thing. Once something arrives here, it's dead. Whatever life it had before, it's dead now. A lot of them – we don't know who they are. There's a box of skulls with bullet holes in them and that's all we know. Things like that. If there were documents or information acquired with objects at the time of their arrival that didn't fit their understanding of things in that time period, the museum just got rid of the documents.'

She moves toward the earth to catch her breath.

I think of Mahomet. How lucky he is to at least be in the ground. Not on a shelf or display case. That we were able to bring him a bit of home since he can't be returned to be buried with his ancestors.

The man makes an attempt at comforting, 'Don't worry though, they haven't *displayed* any of the Native American human remains for at least a decade now.'

Then why don't you let them come home?

When I was growing up my mom was constantly working on repatriation claims, I'd find her laying awake at night worried about our relatives locked up in strange places. The times they were returned, those spirits and their bodies would pass through our home on their way back to the ground. *These are our families*. If you aren't even displaying them, what possible reason could you have to keep them?

'They don't know what returning them would set a precedent for.'

But they've set precedents for far worse things before.
That's a decision made out of fear. Wouldn't it be nice –
if the precedent setting was about care for other people,
setting precedents for healing instead of trauma?

'Yes, yes, we all agree. Oh, I wanted to show you – there is a
drum! The only acknowledgement of African Americans in
the museum, because the institution does not document
what it terms "hybrid cultures." The bottom of the drum is
made from wood from Africa and the top is made from a
deer hide in North America,' he excitedly explains.

*She is losing the ability to navigate between the two characters, as the
effect of his words on her is growing.*

'Oh, and somewhere in the stocks is a whip made from a
Sioux hip bone.'

I wander away, and stare at an exhibit on clocks for a while,
wishing I could cleanse my body of all the stolen stories and
objects of violence in this place.

I want to go home.

I don't want to be the Native American in front of the word
Shakespeare.

Just another kind of display case filled with things too
complicated to be understood by those not listening hard
enough to the ancestors speaking through it.

Everyone freaked out when they discovered Shakespeare's
head might be missing, but no one cares how many Native
skulls sit in boxes unlabeled.[30]

---

[30] The estimate of 12,000 was given to me in real time by a former employee of the
museum during this interaction. The British Museum publicly admits to at least 6,000
on its website, some of which are groupings of remains. The obsession with holding
onto Native remains in the US is ongoing. A recent article in *Smithsonian Magazine*,
titled 'When Museums Rushed to Fill Their Rooms with Bones,' estimated the number
of Native American Remains in American museums as a whole to be about 500,000.

I'm sorry I have nothing to offer the spirits crowding this building, mashed up against friends, enemies, and strangers who don't understand them. All yearning to go home.

I am scared to close my eyes and listen to the howling and pain around me.

She closes her eyes, and tries to soothe them.

Shhhhh . . .

I certainly didn't bring enough tobacco . . .

Or cedar, sage, and sweetgrass in this case . . .

'You may not believe me, but this place is haunted' – he goes on . . .

You don't say . . .

Breaking Point[31]

As she moves through this section the lines around her increase until they form a box amidst which she is trapped.

I fly. I fly. I land.

I open the feedback on my most recent PhD update: 'While the *passion* behind this writing is evident, we would appreciate a *cooler* rewrite.'

I fly. I fly. I land.

I'm on a bus, I'm on a bus, I'm on a bus, driving along a border.
They. Us. Them. Whose. A border. Someone made another border. Fly. Land. Border.
So many lines in the same place.
Whose box am I in?
'We would appreciate a cooler rewrite, a more distanced, analytical approach to the work.'

---

[31] An alternative version of the scene breaking point was performed both at The Globe in 2019, and in the film adaptation in 2021, from what is in the tour. The text is included at the end of this script for reference.

What does that even mean?
'Distanced, analytical.'
Is that –
'As an academic it's your job to define, to separate, to draw lines between –'
I can't do that – don't you see that's part of the –
'Academia is about critique.'
Why would I –
'You need to be able to judge, to set yourself apart without emotion.'
But that's how –
'One individual.'
There's no such thing –
'Objective.'
Object. Object. Object.
'Without emotion.'

Amidst the encroaching voices and lines there is a moment of stillness.

When my mother was born, my grandmother cried because she had blue eyes . . . and that meant there would be no more Mohegan people. The apocalypse come again. But we are still here . . . what makes us who we are?

VOICEOVER: we must all stand in love for the tribe.

'So next draft –'

I can't!
I can't do what you want me to do!
I'm sorry.
I quit.

I fly. I land.

I need to go home.

I fly. I land.

A line/border appears.

The line is long, so many people, elders, children, families are being detained aside.

The border guard looks up, 'Where do you live?'

Mohegan. Uh, Connecticut?

'What were you doing?'

Working on a PhD.

'Did you complete your studies?'

Uh, no . . .

The border guard hands me back my passport. 'Welcome home.'

She steps over/through the line.

You'd think they can't keep Native Americans out. But try telling that to the Indigenous nations whose territories fall on both sides of the border to Mexico. They predate the US constitution, and still a wall will be built . . . to divide us. Sometimes, I wonder where they think we're supposed to go . . .

My feet don't fall quite right when I land. Maybe I left something behind . . .

I'm not sure what.

But I'm home.

Home?

Real Indians

I'm at a bachelorette party. It's at my tribe's casino on our reservation.
No, not all tribes have casinos.
Mine does.
We're at Mohegan Sun, when one of the girls I don't know says:

'The first time I came to the casino I was so obsessed with finding a Mohegan to take a picture with. And I finally found one in the elevator just as I was leaving! I was so thrilled! I still have the picture.'

I listen.
Frozen.
I don't speak.
I'm here.
I'm at home.
I know I should speak.
It's my job to speak.
Speak. Come on. Speak.
What am I waiting for?
Make them understand.
It's your job to make them understand.

But instead one of the other girls replies:

'I grew up down the road. There are actually a lot more Native people around here than you realize. They don't all look the same. I loved growing up here because my house, it's not just near the casino, which is fun, but also Fort Shantok, their sacred lands, are right down the road. That's where they have their wigwam festival every year, where there's dancing, stories, and oh my god such good food. Mmmm. Every time I go, I get to learn something new about the culture of this place and the people whose lands we're standing on, y'know?'

'So they're, like, legit?' The other girl asks.

'Ya, they're definitely legit. And you shouldn't be treating them like zoo animals. Not everyone wants their picture taken.'

Someone else said something.
It's ridiculous
But
When
In all my life

When?
Is this the first time?
When
In my life
Has a non-Native person
Ever been the one to say something?
To defend us
Even lightly
To treat us like people too . . .
Could they have done this the whole time?

More Bird Than Wolf

I fly
I fly
I fly

Where am I going? Can someone tell me where I'm going?

The world is very dark.

Can you come home, once you cross the ocean?
Does the ocean take some of your spirit?
Does the sky?
Does your language?
Does being treated fairly and then unfairly make you realize
that across each line the rules are different and all of them
have been made up.

Where is the place I can go? Somewhere beyond? Like
Occom did, to escape the poisons of this world? Where can
we go to start over?

She desperately searches for where she can go.

I fly. I land.

The strangest of all British customs to me is their distance
from colonialism. I don't think they realize what they do.
They were thrilled when I arrived as a Native Shakespeare

scholar because they thought that meant Native people *chose* Shakespeare as superior.

I might love him, but I didn't choose him.

He is what I have to live through, in a world that would prefer there be a *last* of the Mohegans.

No one writes the story of Uncas' children.
Because admitting Uncas' children means he survives.
Means he's real.
And everything that happened to him
is still happening.
Every day.
No one writes the story of
Mahomet
Gladys
Flying Bird
Why would they?
They're still too concerned with winning.
They still don't understand that no one wins wars.
No one wins wars.
So they shout
LAST
LAST
LAST
over and over again,
until it's the only word people recognize associated with
Mohegan.
And we grow up even asking ourselves if we exist?
If we're allowed to exist?
Where?
Where can I exist?
But the sky?

Shakespeare is a weapon.
So I picked it up and tried to wield it
I truly believed that maybe, maybe if in the twenty-first
century there was a Mohegan girl, the descendant of
generations of chiefs and medicine people, that was a

Shakespeare director, that that would mean something –
But who does it mean something to?
Who do we mean something to?
Do I mean something to?

No! no, no, no no –
You don't get to be sad.
You don't get to remember me as sad.
There is so much more you can't see.
If I can just find somewhere that I can land
That's safe to land.
I will show you how our stories,
the stories you didn't know, had value
These stories can change how you see the world.
Change what is possible.
Heal you.

Yes, I could *try* to show you with Shakespeare
Bend the words of a four-hundred-year-old English poet
Who never saw outside his Christian monarchy
To pretend he understood more than he did
That's what you want, isn't it?
For me to show you how his words are *universal*
Those few words written at a time
When we still had ours
All of *ours*
Our Words
We still had all *our words*
But every single one of his
Even the ones he made up
Even the ones that meant nothing
You gave value
You saved
Treasured
Cared for
But ours
You tore from our throats and you threw them away
Because you did not understand them.

And what a waste.
What an incredible waste.
That I can't tell you the story you need to hear right now.
Because we can't speak it together.
We can't listen to the language made up of the earth under
our feet.
The stories it whispers.
The lessons it needs to hear.
To heal.
No, I'm not sad.
It's not sad for me.
It's a waste
For all of us.
For humanity not to have the words it needs right now
to survive.
So what do we do?

She searches.

Ancestors, where do I go?
Where can I go?

The sky.

She begins her transformation.

Close your eyes.
You are a bird.
The wind under your wings.
The turbulence, the support of your ancestors carrying you.

I've been trying to remember a story . . .
Can you help me?
A long time ago our ancestors told it to us . . .
I think it has to do with where we belong.

I went up in the sky to help my people,
but the sky,
I don't want to let it go . . .
How far away I am. How much the bird I was named for.
The one who flies apart.

A messenger between the spirit world and our own.
Not just any bird, but a blackbird.
A bird just common enough to move between cultures
unnoticed.
As I fly – a current of spirits asks me questions, tells me
stories, riding wind.

I take them with me, each time I fly –
the ancestors of the earth I'm made of,
the water that carried them,
and the spirit wind that carries me.
You don't get to trap a tempest.
The earth will make its way somehow with or without us.
In the sky the borders disappear.

I look
down
down
down
at the wide world,
at the wolves,
at the people.
They want me to tell them somewhere is better.
Each time I fly.
As if it's that simple.
As if we can perch in a distant future where every problem
we have is answered,
as if I can fly somewhere where I am supposed to exist.

But the bird with no language didn't find such an easy
answer.
Fly. Perch. Fly.
More and more trouble staying grounded.
Fly. Perch. Fly.
She realized what she could see was different, from each tree
she landed in.
Each ancestor told her to land in a different tree.
This was her form now.

She was part of the sky.
It had taken some of her spirit.

As she speaks, these voices are multiplied and magnified around her,
pulling her back down to the earth.

Come back down Acokayis.
Be less Native. Be more Native.
Where are your borders? You need borders.
We will get a new neverland and build it new borders.
How come you don't hate? How come you don't hate? How
come you don't hate?
Talk about *The Tempest*. *The Tempest*. *The Tempest*. Talk about
the – Talk about the. Talk about the – Why can't you hate?

shhhhhh

The sounds cut out as she rises up beyond the world around her and
her perspective completely transforms.

Keesuq.[32]
Keesuq.
Keesuq.

We are so very far beyond the Earth now, and together we see the
world as we only can from the sky.

They don't see.

They don't see.
I'm a bird.

So I couldn't tell them.
I couldn't tell them what I saw.
Not in a way they could understand it from down below.
From the sky one world might be clear,
but the closer you get to something,
it is always more complicated on the ground.

Earth crashes in.

---

[32] Translation: Sky.

Fear Of Landing

'Are you coming to the tribal graduation ceremony?' Mom asks.

What do you mean? I didn't graduate.

'You got another Masters.'

Yeah, but you know what I mean, I quit my PhD it will be embarrassing.

'I think it will be good. It is good to celebrate these things.'

But I quit. I quit. It will be weird.

'Did you learn something? . . . Shantok, tomorrow night. I think your grandma would like you to go.'

She steps into the world of Shantok, it is green, open, and has the natural sounds of home.

I take a slow stroll through Shantok. Uncas' village, our burial ground. Surrounded by ancestors, generations of wolves. Uncas, Lucy, Flying Bird, Gladys. They are all here with me, watching, listening.

I wish Mahomet was here – but we can't bring him back from London. Our spirits are stretched and torn too far.

She steps forward.

I am standing in a queue – to graduate. With cousins.

All the Mohegans completing a degree this year. Funds from our casino are used to ensure we all have free education, so the line is long. The U.S. may not have good education policies, but our sovereign Mohegan nation does.

I feel like I am waiting in line to get in trouble.

One of my cousins gives me a big celebratory hug, 'Hey, I didn't know you were graduating this year, what are you graduating from?'

I got a degree in Shakespeare . . .

. . . And as I say it, I realize it's true.

What about you?

In the line is each person graduating, and the relative who will honor them. Excited to be the ones chosen to speak about the graduates they are so proud of. Mom's not in the line with me. As Medicine Woman, she's overseeing the event.

When I get to the front, there is silence.
I am terrified.
That all my cousins will know somehow,
that I didn't complete something,
that I did something wrong,
that I am too much bird now,
that I don't belong.
But when I get to the front of the line. Mom says:

'In the weeks before she was born, the house filled up with birds – and so I chose to name her Blackbird after Flying bird, because it was blackbirds that had filled the house. She has always been a free spirit and an independent person, and the name suited her, but I was still surprised when she decided to fly across the sea and pursue a degree in Shakespeare, and make that same journey that Samson Occom and Mahomet made before her.
It worries us when people leave, because we're afraid that when they leave, they won't come home. That their spirits will get trapped somewhere else – and we will have to spend generations just trying to get them back, back home to Mohegan. But sometimes to leave, means building relationships with other nations, means opening up to new ways of seeing the world, means more paths that future Mohegans can travel, knowing their ancestors are still at their back.

We named her blackbird, because we knew she would have to fly. And each time she does she learns something she brings back to all of us.'

Epilogue: Everywhere[33]

We can't gather as a tribe like that now.
Flying is not so easy either.
Week by week we don't know what will be off limits.
The sky.
The land.
The river.
This. (*Indicating the theater.*)
Place is different. Time is different.
People are different.
Words mean more.

What if I couldn't call my mother?
What if our elders were taken from us?
All at once.
Would we have listened hard enough?
Would I have listened hard enough to what I was supposed
to learn?
Or would that knowledge be lost forever?

A sacred relation came home this year.
The surviving journals[34] of Flying Bird
the last fluent speaker of the Mohegan language.
They came home.

We know these objects carry the spirits of our relations.
So it's as if Flying Bird truly came home herself,

---

[33] The Epilogue changes per production to bring us into the moment in time of the story's telling. This version of the Epilogue is from Fall 2021. The version performed at The Globe in 2019, there was no epilogue and the play ended with graduation. The film version recorded in April 2021 before most people had been vaccinated against Covid-19 started with:
It's been a long time since I've seen a border
The sky's off limits now.
Yet I find myself in many countries at once
Without a need for wings.
Place is different. Time is different.
People are different.
Words mean more

[34] All of Fidelia Fielding's diaries were thought to be destroyed in a fire at the home of Columbia University linguist John Dyneley Prince in the early twentieth century. But her son found more diaries after Fidelia's passing, while he was in quarantine during the pandemic of 1918.

in these pages of her words,
our words,
our language.
Her hope for our future.
Returned from the university that held them.[35]

Our language came home
To teach our children
Our grandchildren
So that one day
My descendents will write plays,
tell stories,
Carry their names
Speak to the ancestors
in our language once more.

The institution let her come home.
They always can.
You just have to decide it's okay to let go
To hold on less tightly, release what isn't yours
To listen
To care.
Our planet is so small.
When will we learn we're all responsible for each other?

She welcomes each of the ancestors into the space.

Wigwomun Jeets Bodernasha!
Wigwomun Uncas!
Wigwomun Skeedumbak Nonner!
Wigwomun Mahomet Weyonomon!
Wigwomun!
Wigwomun!
(*She sings.*) Wigwomun, wigwomun wami skeetôpák, oh hai,
oh hai, heyuh heyuh, weyuh hey.[36]

She thanks the ancestors. End of Play.

---

[35] The surviving journals of Flying Bird were repatriated by the Mohegan Tribe from Cornell University in 2021.

[36] This is a Mohegan Welcoming Song created by the Unity of Nations drum group, under then-drumkeeper, now Council of Elders Chair Charles 'Two Bears' Strickland.

Alternative Version of the Beginning of BREAKING POINT from Film Adaptation[37]

I fly. I fly. I land.

Where am I going?   .
Can someone tell me where I am going?

I fly. I fly. I land.

I open the feedback on my most recent PhD update: 'While the passion behind this writing is evident, we would appreciate a *cooler* rewrite.'
I fly. I fly. I land.
I'm on a bus. I'm on a bus. I'm on a bus.
Driving along a border.
My friend is telling me about his organization, he brings Israelis and Palestinians together to play backgammon.
It brings people together to face each other,
to humanize each other.
People. People. Just people.
I'm on a bus driving along the
Israeli
Palestinian
border.
Another border. A border that was made. We make borders.
People.
Creating so much violence for those who have to contend with it.

Fight over it. Die over it. And the rest of the world yells and howls, and it doesn't solve anything. So he brings people together to play backgammon.
To compete, face to face. The us vs. them is still there,
But it's different somehow, over a game of backgammon . . .

---

[37] I quit my PhD while on a bus in Israel/Palestine. The first version of this scene reflected the specificity of how that happened. I was incredibly angry that the British Empire's tendency to draw lines wherever it pleases, has destroyed generations of lives across the world. I needed to return to working with people. I didn't want to see the world from an academic lens. Later, I changed the scene so that it could build more directly on what happens in The British Museum and better reflect the state of confusion I was still in at that moment.

When my mother was born, my grandmother cried because she had blue eyes . . . and that meant there would be no more Mohegan people. The apocalypse come again. But we are still here . . . what makes us who we are?

As we drive along the border, the border, the border, so many borders,
a friend is telling me about when he quit his PhD program – hang on one second I say,
looking at the spare pathetic fence defining a bloody line across land,
I need to send an email.

She looks down.

Sorry.

She looks back up.

I had to quit my PhD.

I need to work with living people again.

I fly. I land.

I need to go home.

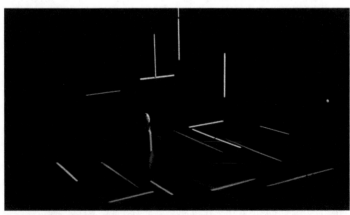

Image by jb.